Seven Last Words
of Christ from the Cross

A Devotional Bible Study and Meditation
on the Passion of Christ for Holy Week,
Maundy Thursday, and
Good Friday Services

For Personal Use, Small Groups or
Sunday School Classes, and Sermon Preparation for
Pastors and Teachers

JesusWalk® Bible Study Series

Ralph F. Wilson
Director, Joyful Heart Renewal Ministries

Free Question Handout Sheets
www.jesuswalk.com/7-last-words/7-last-words-questions.pdf

JesusWalk® Publications
www.jesuswalk.com/books/
Loomis, California

ISBN-13: 978-0-9819721-2-1
ISBN-10: 0981972128

Library of Congress Control Number: 2009912260

Library of Congress subject headings:

> Jesus Christ – Seven last words
> Jesus Christ – Seven last words – Sermons
> Good Friday
> Jesus Christ – Passion
> Jesus Christ – Crucifixion
> Crucifixion of the Christ
> Holy Week
> Holy Week – Meditations

Suggested Classifications:

> Library of Congress: BT455 - BT457
> Dewey Decimal: 232.96

Published by JesusWalk® Publications, P.O. Box 565,
Loomis, CA 95650, USA.   JesusWalk.com

JesusWalk is a registered trademark and Joyful Heart is a
trademark of Joyful Heart Renewal Ministries.

Unless otherwise stated, quotations are from the New
International Version (International Bible Society, 1973,
1978, 1983). Used by permission.

091113   1.0

Preface

James J. Tissot, "The Earthquake" (1886-1894), opaque watercolor, Brooklyn Museum.

By all accounts Jesus didn't do a lot of talking on the cross. He was silent during the hours he hung there, except for a very few words. But these Seven Last Words provide a window into Jesus' soul, a way to understand what is ultimately important to this One who is dying on the cross.

As I have studied and meditated on each Word, trying to plumb the meaning of each saying, I have been touched by the awe of the scene on Golgotha that dark, foreboding Friday afternoon as Jesus hung on the cross. I've learned, I think, to understand him better – his incredible love, his determination, his humanness as well as his divinity, his intimate relationship with his Father, and finally his trust.

It isn't often that we can see with such clarity into a human being, especially Jesus the Son of God himself. But the looking inspires in us awe and changes us forever.

I encourage you to study these Seven Last Words one each day in a single week. The best might be during Holy Week, beginning on the Saturday before Palm Sunday and finishing on Good Friday itself. Some of you will use these meditations as the basis for a Good Friday service.

However you use them, don't rush through them. Let each of them simmer on the stove of your heart for a while so all the flavors begin to meld together into a unique and satisfying aroma.

Some are longer than others. I resisted the temptation to make them all the same length as if they were all equally significant. So savor all of these Seven Last Words from the cross, both the long and the short, that you may encounter Christ in them.

Spend some time thinking about the question for personal meditation that concludes each of the Words. In framing an answer, you'll find yourself stretched and sharpened as you begin to put into your own words thoughts that have remained only fuzzy in your mind until now.

I have illustrated each of these lessons with re-markable watercolors by James Jacques Tissot (1836-1902), a French painter who spent the last two decades of his life visiting the Holy Land twice and producing some 700 illustrations of the Old Testament and the Gospels. I hope you enjoy his work as much as I do. You can view them at larger size online at www.joyfulheart.com/holy-week/

My prayer is that these Seven Last Words of Christ from the Cross will bless you and draw you closer to the One who died for you and to the Father who sent his Son on this costly journey to redeem us.

Dr. Ralph F. Wilson
Loomis, California

References and Abbreviations

BDAG   Walter Bauer and Frederick W. Danker, *A Greek-English Lexicon of the New Testament and Other Early Christian Literature* (Third Edition; based on a previous English edition by W.F. Arndt, F.W. Gingrich, and F.W. Danker; University of Chicago Press, 1957, 1979). This is the standard NT Greek-English Lexicon.

BDB   Francis Brown, S.R. Driver, and Charles A. Briggs, *A Hebrew and English Lexicon of the Old Testament* (Clarendon Press, 1907)

Beasley-   George R. Beasley-Murray, *John* (Word
Murray   Biblical Commentary, vol. 36; Word, 1987)

Death   Raymond E. Brown, *Death of the Messiah* (Doubleday, 1994), volumes 1 and 2.

France   R.T. France, *The Gospel of Matthew* (New International Commentary on the New Testament; Eerdmans, 2007)

ISBE   Geoffrey W. Bromiley (general editor), *The*

International Standard Bible Encyclopedia (Eerdmans, 1979-1988; fully revised from the 1915 edition)

KJV   King James Version (1611)

Life &   Alfred Edersheim, *The Life and Times of*
Times   *Jesus the Messiah* (2 volume edition; Eerdmans, 1969, reprinted from the third edition, 1886)

Lane   William L. Lane, *Commentary on the Gospel of Mark* (New International Commentary on the New Testament; Eerdmans, 1974)

Marshall   I. Howard Marshall, *Commentary on Luke* (New International Greek Testament Commentary; Eerdmans, 1978)

Merriam-   *Merriam-Webster's Collegiate Dictionary*
Webster   (Tenth Edition; Merriam-Webster, 1993)

Morris   Leon Morris, *The Gospel According To John* (New International Commentary on the New Testament; Eerdmans, 1971)

NASB   New American Standard Bible (Lockman Foundation, 1971, 1977)

NIDNTT   Colin Brown (general editor), *The New International Dictionary of New Testament*

Theology (Zondervan, 1975-1978; translated with additions and revisions from *Theologisches Begriffslexikon zum Neuen Testament*, 1967-1971, three volume edition)

NIV   New International Version (International Bible Society, 1973, 1978, 1983)

NRSV   New Revised Standard Version (Division of Christian Education of the National Council of Churches of Christ, 1989)

Strack and Billerbeck   H.L. Strack und P. Billerbeck, *Kommentar zum Neuen Testament aus Talmud und Midrasch* (München, 1956)

TDNT   Gerhard Kittel and Gerhard Friedrich (editors), Geoffrey W. Bromiley (translator and editor), *Theological Dictionary of the New Testament* (Eerdmans, 1964-1976; translated from *Theologisches Wörterbuch zum Neuen Testament*, ten volume edition)

Thayer   Joseph Henry Thayer, *Greek-English Lexicon of the New Testament* (Associated Publishers and Authors, n.d., reprinted from 1889 edition, used in electronic form)

Table of Contents

Reprint Guidelines

Copying the Handouts. In some cases, small groups or Sunday school classes would like to use the Participant Guide handouts. That's great. An online file provides copies of the handouts designed for classes and small groups. There is no charge whatsoever to print out as many copies of the handouts as you need for participants. They can be found at:

www.jesuswalk.com/7-last-words/7-last-words-questions.pdf

All charts and notes are copyrighted and must bear the line:

"Copyright © 2009, Ralph F. Wilson. All rights reserved. Reprinted by permission."

You may not resell these notes to other groups or individuals outside your congregation. You may, however, charge people in your group enough to cover your copying costs.

Copying the book (or the majority of it). If you copy the book for your congregation or group, you are requested to purchase a reprint license for each book. For better copies, I recommend that you reprint the e-book version, not the paperback version. A Reprint License, $2.50 for each copy, is available for purchase at:

www.jesuswalk.com/books/7-last words.htm

Or you may send a check to:

> Dr. Ralph F. Wilson
> Joyful Heart Renewal Ministries
> PO Box 308
> Rocklin, CA 95677, USA

The Scripture says,

> "The laborer is worthy of his hire" (Luke 10:7) and "Anyone who receives instruction in the word must share all good things with his instructor" (Galatians 6:6).

However, if you are from a third world country or an area where it is difficult to transmit money, please make a small contribution instead to help the poor in your community.

1. Father, Forgive Them (Luke 23:34)

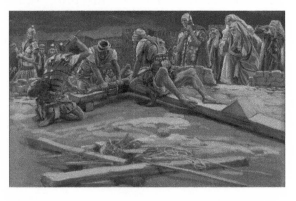

James J. Tissot, "The First Nail" (1886-1894), opaque watercolor, Brooklyn Museum.

"³² Two other men, both criminals, were also led out with him to be executed. ³³ When they came to the place called the Skull, there they crucified him, along with the criminals – one on his right, the other on his left. ³⁴ Jesus said, **'Father, forgive them, for they do not know what they are doing.'** And they divided up his clothes by casting lots." (Luke 23:32-34)

The scene around the cross is crass and unfeeling. The soldiers are part of an execution detail, bored with crucifixion. Perhaps this team will have conducted several crucifixions this week already. The first time they saw a crucifixion they may have been moved by its brutality, but now they are calloused, emotionless.

First, the soldiers begin with the cruel process of nailing the criminal to a cross, then hoisting him up, the cross swaying forward, then back until it is secured with wedges at the bottom to hold it upright in the hole. And when that task is done, they sit around the base waiting for the criminal to die – sometimes for days. To pass the time they gamble, deciding by a casting of lots who will be awarded the victim's last possessions. That is the scene.

But in the midst of it comes an astounding, powerful word from the "criminal" on the center cross:

> "Father, forgive them, for they do not know what they are doing." (Luke 23:34a)

An Unselfish Prayer

Stop reading silently for a moment and speak this sentence out loud and listen to yourself as you say the words:

> "Father, forgive them, for they do not know what they are doing." (Luke 23:34a)

What is Jesus saying? In his last hour, Jesus is saying a prayer, a request to God Almighty. It is remarkable, however, that Jesus isn't asking for himself! I would be terrified and overwhelmed, trying desperately to retain my composure. My prayer would probably be: "God help me!" if I could utter any sounds at all.

But Jesus' prayer is one of complete unselfishness. He is concerned for the people who are responsible for crucifying him and is asking God to forgive them. Instead of thinking of himself and his own needs, he is thinking of those whose souls are in much greater peril than his own. The first thing I learn from this word is love. At his last extremity, Jesus loves.

Father – a term of trust, confidence, and endearment

But his love is not merely for those base military functionaries who put him on the cross. His prayer reveals a gentle love for God himself. At the moment he begins the long course of death through excruciating pain, he speaks in love to the only One who can deliver him – God himself! He speaks not for himself, but for others. And he speaks in love.

Think about the word "Father" in this prayer and consider the alternatives.

"God" is the generic term for deity.

"Lord" is a term of respect and honor for one who is exalted in rank. This term was substituted by the Jews to avoid saying the divine name of Yahweh or Jehovah when reading the Scripture.

"Almighty God" would be a bit formal at the desperate hour of one's crucifixion, but it would express God's great power.

"Creator God" is a common substitute for "Father" among Christians who want to avoid the paternalism they see in the word "Father." But "Creator God" is not a term of relationship, rather one of function and awe.

"Father," on the other hand, is first and foremost a term of relationship and endearment. It is a family term. Spoken within the family circle it was often expressed as "Abba," which, roughly translated, might correspond to our "Dad" or "Daddy." Jesus had used this intimate Aramaic word to address his Father in the Garden of Gethsemane the night before (Mark 14:36). It is also the cry of the Spirit of God within us, helping us reach out to God (Romans 8:15; Galatians 4:6).

In this prayer at his last hour, Jesus addresses the God of the Universe with the simple term "Father." And he invites us to do the same. When Jesus' disciples ask him how they should pray, he gives them a model prayer that begins, "Our Father..." (Matthew 6:9).

By beginning his prayer with the word "Father," Jesus expresses at the same time a love and a confidence, a trust. One who doubts might pile up descriptors of God to buttress his shaky faith, but one who calls him simply, "Father," knows him, trusts him, and is confident in the outcome.

Who Does the "Them" Refer To?

Consider the prayer again:

> "Father, forgive **them**, for **they** do not know what **they** are doing." (Luke 23:34a)

Jesus prays that the Father would forgive "them." Who are "they" for whom he prays? Let's consider the possibilities.

Soldiers. He could be praying for the Roman soldiers who routinely put men to death on this site of Golgotha. They destroyed a human life, brutally, without compassion, but they didn't initiate the action. They had no choice. They were merely following orders. Only after the fact did they realize with awe and terror what they had done: "Surely he was the Son of God!" said the centurion (Matthew 27:54). It could have been the soldiers he was forgiving.

Pilate, however, might have been a better candidate. Against all law he had given the order for the crucifixion. He had found Jesus innocent of the crimes with which he had been charged. Yet, the pressure of the Jewish leaders and his fear of a riot "forced" him to go against his own better judgment. He signed the death warrant and then publically washed his hands (Matthew 27:24) – the crass, double-faced act of a self-serving politician desperate to hold onto power. Perhaps Jesus was forgiving Pilate for the weakness of his character.

Chief priests and scribes were the prime force behind the crucifixion. Once Jesus had cleansed the temple of their greedy trade in animals and money changing at outrageous exchange rates, they were determined to kill him (Matthew 21:15, 23, 45-46; 26:3-4). Behind the scenes they had paid off Judas for his insider betrayal (Matthew 26:14-16), sent temple soldiers to arrest Jesus in the Garden of Gethsemane (Matthew 26:47), tried to get people to testify falsely against him before the Sanhedrin (Matthew 26:59), brought his case before Pilate (Matthew 27:1-2), and stirred up the crowd to demand that Jesus be crucified (Matthew 27:20-23). It may have been the chief priests and scribes that Jesus was forgiving.

Pharisees and Sadducees were his early enemies. Jesus' plain teaching about the Kingdom of God offended them both. The Sadducees sought to discredit him (Matthew 22:23-34). The Pharisees were the first to actively plot Jesus' death (Matthew 12:14). I would guess that if Jesus came to our churches today, many of our leaders would oppose him openly. Some might plot to destroy him. The real Jesus is just too threatening to established religious power that resists change. It might be the Pharisees and Sadducees who were the recipients of his plea for mercy.

You and I. But when you think about it, we are the real ones that sent Jesus to the cross – our sins, our corruption, our weakness and pettiness. The way we're headed on our own is to our doom – that's what Jesus says. The gate to eternal life is exceedingly narrow, he tells us – so narrow that few find it on their own (Matthew 7:13-14). Without Jesus' active campaign to bear our sins upon himself, the Righteous for the unrighteous (1 Peter 3:18), none of us could be forgiven.

Jesus is under no illusions. He knows why he has come to earth. He explains it with utmost clarity to his disciples:

> "For even the Son of Man did not come to be served, but to serve, and to give his life as a ransom for many." (Mark 10:45)

You and I made the cross necessary. We are the ones he prays to forgive.

Did We Know What We Were Doing?

Are people forgiven only if they don't know what they are doing? Jesus says,

> "Father, forgive them, for they do not know what they are doing." (Luke 23:34a)

Does God hold those who put Jesus to death responsible for their sins? Oh, yes. He is a just God. They had seen Jesus' miracles and heard the truth spoken by the Son of God himself and had yet sought his death. There was plenty of rope to justly hang them with all.

Yes, they knew this was a dirty business. Their hearts were corrupt. But what was lacking was a full understanding of the magnitude of their sin. That they lacked. Paul explains:

> "None of the rulers of this age **understood** it, for if they had, they would not have crucified the Lord of glory." (1 Corinthians 2:8; see Acts 3:17)

Paul himself, who persecuted Christians to their death, did it because he just didn't understand.

> "Even though I was once a blasphemer and a persecutor and a violent man, I was shown mercy because I acted in **ignorance and unbelief**." (1 Timothy 1:13)

What I learn from this First Word is that God is merciful – far more merciful than any of us deserves. Yes, each of us has more than enough sin to condemn us. But God is looking deeper. He has made a way that we do not deserve, because he knows that if we really knew the truth, we would embrace his Son.

Jesus' prayer on the cross tells me that God has found a way to forgive us.

What Does It Mean to Forgive?

This leads me to the last question raised by this saying: What does it mean to forgive?

The word in Greek is *aphiēmi*, with the basic meaning of "to send away." The word occurs often in Greek commercial papyrus fragments of the time with the idea of "to release from legal or moral obligation or consequence, cancel, remit, pardon."[1] The word was used in legal documents to describe releasing a person from an office, severing a marriage obligation, or cancelling a debt that was owed.[2]

In the Lord's Prayer Jesus uses the verb *aphiēmi* in the context of debt:

> "And forgive us our debts, as we forgive our
> debtors." (Matthew 6:12)

He is speaking of sins as a debt owed to God which must be paid. The Lord's Prayer asks God to cancel our debts – as we cancel others' debt of sins committed against us. In the Parable of the Unforgiving Servant (Matthew 18:23-35) Jesus illustrates the concept of forgiveness in terms of a massive financial debt owed to a king.

There's a song by Ellis J. Crum that expresses the concept of God's forgiveness rather succinctly:

> "He paid a debt He did not owe,
> I owed a debt I could not pay,
> I needed someone to wash my sin away.
> And now I sing that brand new song:
>   Amazing Grace,

---

[1] *Aphiēmi*, BDAG 156, 2.
[2] Rudolf Bultmann, *aphiēmi, ktl.*, TDNT 1:509-512.

For Jesus paid the debt
that I could never pay."[3]

That pretty well says it all.

As Jesus begins the last phase of his life – dying on a cross hung between earth and heaven – he prays for all of us who put him there. He calls out to his Father, without any shame at the intimacy of his love and the authenticity of his Sonship – "Father, forgive them." And so we pray the prayer ourselves: Father, forgive us.

Prayer

Yes, Father, forgive us. We really didn't know the depths to which we have fallen. And we are just coming to realize the depth of the love you have for us – and have always had. Cancel our debt of sin to you, we pray. Not because we deserve it, but out of your great mercy revealed by the cross. For we pray this in the Name of Jesus who died on that cross to bring about just this result. Amen!

Question for Personal Meditation

Q1. (Luke 23:34) Who was most responsible for killing Jesus? What responsibility do you and I bear in this? In what sense was Jesus praying for us?
http://www.joyfulheart.com/forums/index.php?showtopic=879

---

[3] "He Paid a Debt He Did Not Owe," words and music by Ellis J. Crum (© 1977, Ellis J. Crum, Publisher; admin. by Sacred Music, a Trust).

Questions for Group Discussion

1. What term do you usually use to address God? Why? How might your faith be affected if you started addressing God in your prayers as "Father"? How would it help you better understand the relationship between you and God?

2. In what sense can your sin be seen as a debt owed to God? How do you pay off a debt like that? On what just basis can God forgive this debt of sin?

3. What does knowledge of sin have to do with Jesus' forgiveness? At what level did Jesus' killers understand what they were doing?

4. Who was most responsible for killing Jesus? What responsibility do we bear for Jesus' death on the cross?

2. This Day You Will Be with Me in Paradise (Luke 23:43)

"³⁹ One of the criminals who hung there hurled insults at him: 'Aren't you the Christ? Save yourself and us!' ⁴⁰ But the other criminal rebuked him. 'Don't you fear God,' he said, 'since you are under the same sentence? ⁴¹ We are punished justly, for we are getting what our deeds deserve. But this man has done nothing wrong.' ⁴² Then he said, 'Jesus, remember me when you come into your kingdom.' ⁴³ Jesus answered him, 'I tell you the truth, today you will be with me in paradise.'" (Luke 23:39-43)

James J. Tissot, "Pardoning of the Good Thief" (1886-1894), opaque watercolor, Brooklyn Museum.

It was a terrible thing to be unjustly condemned to be crucified. It added insult to injury to be crucified between two obvious criminals. But there's a story here and a lesson. This brief passage relates one of the most amazing prayers and promises in the entire Bible.

Scripture Is Fulfilled

Before we get into the story, however, it's important to realize that Jesus' crucifixion with other criminals was no accident of history. It is a fulfillment of prophecy:

> "He was assigned a grave with the **wicked**,
> and with the rich in his death,
> though he had done no violence,
> nor was any deceit in his mouth....
> He poured out his life unto death,
> and was **numbered with the transgressors**.
> For he bore the sin of many,
> and made intercession for the transgressors."
> (Isaiah 53:9, 12)

Angry Insults from a Dying Criminal

Hanging on crosses at Jesus' right and left hand are two criminals, Greek *kakourgos*, "criminal, evildoer," one who commits gross misdeeds and serious crimes.[1] Other gospel writers use the term *lestes*,

---

[1] *Kakourgos*, BDAG 502.

"robber, highwayman, bandit"[2] (Matthew 27:38; Mark 15:27).[3]

Though they could have been common thieves, they also might be the kind of highwaymen that swoop down on lonely groups of travelers from Jerusalem to Jericho, strip them of their possessions, and leave them for dead, as in the case of the victim in the Parable of the Good Samaritan (Luke 10:25-37). The same Greek word is used to describe them. Bandits like these two are the terror of travelers.

One of these highwaymen, dying on a cross beside Jesus, now takes up the cat-calling begun by the soldiers, "You are the Christ, aren't you? Then save yourself and us!" It was probably much like the cruel teasing of inmates that goes on in prisons today. It is a jab at authority of any kind, a pulling of everyone down to your own level. The thief is making fun of Jesus' inability to do anything despite the exalted title of "Messiah." Where is this talk of "Messiah" now? he sneers. You're dying just like us. Death is the great equalizer.

The verb used for describing the thief's taunts is *blasphēmeō*, "to speak in a disrespectful way that

[2] *Lestes*, BDAG 594, 1.

[3] The word is also used to describe a "revolutionary, insurrectionist, guerrilla" (BDAG, 594, 2; Mark 15:7; John 18:40), which would have been considered high treason. However, it is clear from evidence cited by Hengel (Martin Hengel, John Bowden (translator), *Crucifixion in the Ancient World and the Folly of the Message of the Cross* (Fortress Press, 1977) pp. 47-50) that robbers were indeed crucified by the Romans. "Robber" accords better with *kakourgos* than "insurrectionist."

demeans, denigrates, maligns. Slander, revile, defame."[4]

The reason this is happening is not only because the thief is wicked, but also in order that the scripture may be fulfilled:

"He was **despised** and **rejected** by men,
a man of sorrows,
   and familiar with suffering.
Like one from whom men hide their faces
   he was **despised**,
and we esteemed him not." (Isaiah 53:3)

"But I am a worm and not a man,
scorned by men and **despised** by the people.
All who see me **mock me**;
they **hurl insults**, shaking their heads:
'He trusts in the LORD;
let the LORD rescue him.
Let him deliver him,
since he delights in him.'" (Psalm 22:6-8)

"Dogs have surrounded me;
a band of evil men has encircled me,
they have pierced my hands and my feet.
I can count all my bones;
people stare and **gloat over me**.
 They divide my garments among them
and cast lots for my clothing."
                                        (Psalm 22:16-18)

---

[4] *Blasphēmeō*, BDAG 178, 1bε.

Just below Jesus' feet the soldiers are casting lots to see who gets his clothing.[5] His last effects aren't given to his family. They go to the soldiers as the "spoils" – also in fulfillment of Scripture (Psalm 22:18). It is the final insult.

This Man Has Done Nothing Wrong

One criminal is blaspheming Jesus, but the other is not.[6]

> "The other criminal rebuked him. 'Don't you fear God,' he said, 'since you are under the same sentence? We are punished justly, for we are getting what our deeds deserve. But this man has done nothing wrong.'" (Luke 23:40-41)

These taunts are making the other condemned brigand very uncomfortable. The word *blasphēmeō* can refer to reviling humans, but also to "speak irreverently, impiously, disrespectfully of or about ... God."[7] The second bandit may be condemned to death, but he has not lost his faith, for he asks, "Don't you fear God?" To stand by and participate in such an unrighteous act as to execute an innocent man is

---

[5] Matthew 27:35b; Mark 15:24b; Luke 23:34b; John 19:23-24.

[6] Or is no longer mocking, after realizing the irony of the situation and who Jesus was (Matthew 27:44; Mark 15:32).

[7] *Blasphēmeō*, BDAG 178, 1bβ.

an impious, sinful act. The second brigand refuses to desert his sense of right and wrong.

Remember Me in Your Kingdom

> "Then he said, 'Jesus, remember me
> when you come into your kingdom.'"
> (Luke 23:42)

By any measure, this statement is astounding! Jesus' disciples have fled or linger disillusioned that dark Friday at the margins of the crowd. Their hopelessness is echoed by the men on the road to Emmaus, "... They crucified him; but we had hoped that he was the one who was going to redeem Israel" (Luke 24:20-21).

But here on the cross, a fellow condemned man, life ebbing out of him, looks to the center cross and sees not another dying man, but the Messiah himself. Somehow, he understands that Jesus is not an impostor and that Jesus will still receive the Kingdom that belongs to the Messiah.

I recall Joseph saying something similar to Pharaoh's cupbearer, prisoner to fellow prisoner, when Joseph predicted that the cupbearer would be released from prison:

> "When all goes well with you, remember me
> and show me kindness; mention me to Pha-
> raoh and get me out of this prison." (Genesis
> 40:14)

How can this quality of faith exist at such a dark time? Already the darkness is falling over the whole land, and yet a dying thief believes.

Did he confess his sins? Yes. "We are punished justly, for we are getting what our deeds deserve" (Luke 23:41). Does he repent? Not verbally, but yes, I think he did. His repentance and hope prompt his plea for mercy, "Remember me...."

Is the Thief Saved?

But was he saved? Jesus commanded baptism. In the longer ending of Mark's Gospel, Jesus says: "Whoever believes and is baptized will be saved, but whoever does not believe will be condemned" (Mark 16:16).[8] But things don't always follow the prescribed order. At the house of Cornelius, for example, the Holy Spirit falls upon Gentiles who believe the words Peter is saying to them. So Peter baptizes them *after* the Holy Spirit comes upon them (Acts 10:44-48).

The key here is faith. The thief on the cross believes; his prayer to Jesus is bursting with faith. He has more faith that day than any other human observing this gruesome scene.

So far as adults are concerned, nearly all Christians would agree that baptism accompanies faith, and should follow faith as soon as appropriate (at least it seems to in all the examples we see in the New

[8] See also Matthew 28:19; Acts 2:38.

Testament), but I would contend that baptism itself
does not save.[9] Paul writes:

> "For it is by grace you have been
> saved, through faith – and this not
> from yourselves, it is the gift of God –
> not by works, so that no one can
> boast." (Ephesians 2:8-9)

We could multiply references to the primacy of
faith, such as, "whosoever believes in him... (John
3:16, 36; 6:40), "your faith has saved you" (Luke 7:50),
and many others. The thief on the cross gives us an
illustration of saving faith that is instructive to us as
we seek to understand this mystery of our salvation.

How about Deathbed Conversions?

The example of the thief on the cross is often cited
as the precedent for deathbed conversions. And so it
is. I don't doubt that the thief had attended one of
Jesus' outdoor teachings and come to "some sort of
faith" there. And so have many who repent and
confess Christ on their deathbeds. The difference
between "some sort of faith" and "saving faith" is
true repentance and the commitment to Christ that
repentance implies.

---

[9] 1 Peter 3:21 is not arguing that baptism saves a person devoid of faith,
but that the baptism itself is an "appeal of a good conscience toward
God" or "the pledge of a good conscience toward God," depending
upon how you interpret the Greek word *eperotema*.

It *is* possible, I believe, to be saved at one's deathbed. But I've seen too many people who say, "I'll follow Christ later. For now I want to have some fun." Some of them don't get a chance to repent on their deathbeds. They die in accidents or from heart attacks, never having a chance to repent at the end of their days. Yes, deathbed salvation is possible – the thief on the cross indicates this – and it may even be real (God only knows the heart), but it must not be relied upon.

Today You'll Be with Me in Paradise

"Jesus answered him, 'I tell you the truth, today you will be with me in paradise.'" (Luke 23:43)

What a wonderful promise Jesus gives to the believing thief: Presence with Christ in paradise! Our English word "paradise" is a transliteration of the Greek word *paradeisos*, which comes from an Old Persian

James J. Tissot, "The Soul of the Penitent Thief" (1886-1894), opaque watercolor, Brooklyn Museum.

word *pairidaeza*, "enclosure, garden."

In the Greek Septuagint translation of the Old Testament the word is used especially for the Garden of God or Garden of Eden in the creation story (Genesis 2:8-10, 16, etc.), thus moving the word from the realm of secular parks to the sacred Garden of God himself. Judaism of Jesus' day equated Paradise with the New Jerusalem and saw it as the present abode of the souls of the departed patriarchs, the elect, and the righteous.[10] In the New Testament the word "paradise" is used three times:

> "Today you will be with me in **paradise**." (Luke 23:43)

> "And I know that this man – whether in the body or apart from the body I do not know, but God knows – was caught up to **paradise**. He heard inexpressible things, things that man is not permitted to tell." (2 Corinthians 12:3-4)

> "He who has an ear, let him hear what the Spirit says to the churches. To him who overcomes, I will give the right to eat from the tree of life, which is in the **paradise** of God." (Revelation 2:7)

In 2 Corinthians 12:3-4, Paul seems to equate the "third heaven" with paradise. I think we can identify

---

[10] *Paradeisos*, BDAG 761. Marshall, *Luke*, p. 872-873. Joachim Jeremias, "*paradeisos*," TDNT 5:765-773.

paradise with heaven and be pretty safe. Jesus is promising the believing thief that he will be with Jesus in heaven "today."

Implications for Soul Sleep

A few Christian groups teach a doctrine known as "soul sleep." Essentially, the doctrine holds that at death the soul "sleeps" and is not conscious until the resurrection. Indeed, there are a number of times when "sleep" is used as a euphemism for death.[11] But three passages make it quite clear that the soul is *not* unconscious until the resurrection:

> "Today you will be with me in paradise." (Luke 23:43)
>
> "We are confident, I say, and would prefer to be away from the body and at home with the Lord." (2 Corinthians 5:8)
>
> "I am torn between the two: I desire to depart and be with Christ, which is better by far." (Philippians 1:23)

Faith and Promise

We know what an encouragement the account of the thief on the cross has been to Christians down through the ages. But how about Jesus, dying alone on the cross? What did it mean to him?

---

[11] Luke 8:52; John 11:11; Acts 7:60; 1 Corinthians 15:18, 20, 51; 1 Thessalonians 4:14-15; 5:10; etc.

I believe the Father blessed his Son with this strange companion during his last hours – a believer, and a very strong believer at that. Jesus had often chaffed at the unbelief he saw around him. His disciples themselves often exhibited "little faith."[12] But occasionally, Jesus encounters someone with great faith. A Roman centurion tells him that he doesn't need to physically come to heal his servant; all he had to do was speak the word and he has authority to have it accomplished (Luke 7:2-10). Jesus is amazed at the man: "I tell you, I have not found such great faith even in Israel" (Luke 7:9).

If you've ever taught, you know how encouraging it is to have a student who grasps what you are trying to communicate. Even if most students fail to understand, at least your prize pupil does, and that brings great satisfaction. The centurion is one of those prize pupils; the thief on the cross is another. Neither is acceptable to religion – one a Gentile, the other a criminal. But each has great faith, and each, I am sure, brings joy to Jesus' heart.

As Jesus dies for our sins, he does not die completely alone. The Father gives him a companion, a believer with mighty faith, a believer who can look past the raw wood and nails and blood to the heavenly kingdom that Jesus will inherit. He is a believer who wants "in." Jesus answers him as life on

---

[12] Luke 12:28; Matthew 8:26; 14:31; 16:8; 17:20.

earth wanes, "Yes, you'll be with me there – today in paradise. We'll go together, you and I."

What a faith!
What a promise!
What a privilege!
What a glory!

Prayer

Father, you never leave yourself without a witness. Even Jesus' close disciples faltered in their faith. But then you raised up a thief who had great faith and received a great promise. Please strengthen my faith. I am often so upset and confused by the buffeting winds of my life. Let me see beyond them to Jesus. By your grace, may my faith bring some joy into your breaking heart as did the thief's faith in Jesus. In Jesus' holy and precious name, I pray. Amen.

Question for Personal Meditation

Q2. (Luke 23:39-43) Why is the thief's faith so astounding in this situation? What did the thief receive that day? What do you think this meant to Jesus?

http://www.joyfulheart.com/forums/index.php?showtopic=880

Questions for Group Discussion

1. Why do you think one of the criminals on the cross insulted and mocked Jesus? What human trait prompted him to do this? (Luke 23:39)

2. Why does the other criminal rebuke him for his insults? On what grounds does he try to stop him? (Luke 23:40-41)

3. What did the thief have to believe about Jesus to cause him to ask him, "Jesus, remember me when you come into your kingdom" (Luke 23:42). What are the elements of his faith?

4. Did the thief confess his sins? Was he repentant?

5. How do you think the thief's request make Jesus feel?

6. What are the elements of Jesus' promise to the thief in Luke 23:43?

7. What are we disciples supposed to learn from this strange exchange on the crosses above our heads? What does Jesus intend for us to get out of this?

3. Woman, Behold Your Son (John 19:26-27)

"²⁵ Near the cross of Jesus stood his mother, his mother's sister, Mary the wife of Clopas, and Mary Magdalene. ²⁶ When Jesus saw his mother there, and the disciple whom he loved standing nearby, he said to his

James J. Tissot, "Mater Dolorosa, Sorrowful Mother" (1889-1896), opaque watercolor, Brooklyn Museum, NYC

mother, **'Dear woman, here is your son,'** ²⁷ and to the disciple, **'Here is your mother.'** From that time on, this disciple took her into his home." (John 19:25-27)

Jesus' Mother at the Foot of the Cross

Of the four gospel writers, John is the only one who records Mary's presence at the cross. But it would be expected that Jesus' mother be in Jerusalem at Passover – after all, we read, "Every year his parents went to Jerusalem for the Feast of the Passover" (Luke 2:41). Probably after Joseph's death – presumed to have taken place before Jesus began his ministry – Mary would come up to Jerusalem for the Feast with friends and relatives.

Now her son is in trouble – arrested, tried, condemned, and now dying. Surely, Mary's place is close to her son. And so Simeon's prophecy given at Jesus' dedication comes to pass:

"And a sword will pierce your own soul too."
(Luke 2:35b)

She is near him now, but her heart is broken. She is consoled by friends.

The Identity of the Other Women

Just who are these friends? Verse 25 seems to include Mary plus three other women.[1] These are probably the same women who appear in the Synoptic Gospels. Matthew explains: "Many women were there, watching from a distance. They had followed Jesus from Galilee to care for his needs" (Matthew 27:55; Luke 8:3).

[1] Some commentators see this as two or three women, but these explanations of the sentence don't make as much sense.

In addition to Mary, the women at the cross seem to be:

John 19:25	Matthew 27:56	Mark 15:40
Jesus' mother's sister	the mother of Zebedee's sons	Salome
Mary (wife) of Clopas	Mary the mother of James and Joses	Mary the mother of James the younger and of Joses
Mary Magdalene	Mary Magdalene	Mary Magdalene

Mary Magdalene is mentioned consistently in all three gospels.

Mary (the wife) of Clopas seems to correspond easily to "Mary the mother of James the younger and of Joses (Joseph)" (Mark 15:40; Matthew 27:56). She is probably "the other Mary" who was with Mary Magdalene at the tomb Friday night and on Sunday morning (Matthew 27:61; 28:1).[2]

---

[2] An early church tradition mentioned by Chrysostom (347-407 AD) identifies Alphaeus, the father of an apostle named James (Matthew 10:3), with this Clopas, father of "James the Less," though this is uncertain. A.W. Fortune, "Alphaeus," ISBE 1:100. Tradition also sees this Alphaeus / Clopas as the brother of St. Joseph (Eusebius, *Church History*, 3.11.2; cf. "Clopas," ISBE 1:724). See also R. Laird Harris, "James (2)," ISBE 2:958-959.

The third woman, **Jesus' mother's sister**, may well be **Salome**, who is the **mother of James and John**, the sons of Zebedee.[3] This would make James and John to be Jesus' cousins. That would make sense. James and John are part of Jesus' inner circle with Peter. It also explains why their mother might presume to ask that her sons sit on Jesus' right and left in his kingdom (Matthew 20:20-21). She had been rebuked by Jesus on that occasion, but here she is at the foot of the cross consoling Mary, Jesus' mother, her sister.

The Disciple Whom Jesus Loved

Now the story unfolds further.

> "[26] When Jesus saw his mother there, and **the disciple whom he loved** standing nearby, he said to his mother, 'Dear woman, here is your son,' [27] and to the disciple, 'Here is your mother.' From that time on, this disciple took her into his home." (John 19:26-27)

Who is this "disciple whom he loved"? We see this phrase only four other times – and only in John's Gospel.[4] This disciple is clearly identified as the author of the Gospel of John (John 21:24). Church tradition[5] identifies this disciple with St. John the

---

[3] See Kathleen E. Corley, "Salome," ISBE 4:286; Beasley-Murray, *John*, p. 348.

[4] John 13:23; 20:2; 21:7; 21:20.

[5] Irenaeus (died 202 AD) writes: "Afterwards, John, the disciple of the Lord, who also had leaned upon His breast, did himself publish a Gospel during his residence at Ephesus in Asia." Irenaeus, *Against*

Apostle. Perhaps the Gospel writer doesn't identify himself by name out of modesty.

This disciple whom Jesus loved, St. John, one of three disciples closest to him, is the only male disciple who is at the foot of the cross as Jesus is dying. The others are too afraid to be so closely identified with a man condemned by the Romans, as well as by the leaders of their own people (Mark 14:50; Luke 23:49). But John is nearby – perhaps to accompany his own mother (Mary's sister).

Woman, Here Is Your Son

"26b He said to his mother, 'Dear woman, here is your son,' 27 and to the disciple, 'Here is your mother.' From that time on, this disciple took her into his home." (John 19:26b-27)

Jesus' Third Word from the cross to this small band

James J. Tissot, "*Sabat Mater* (Woman Behold your Son)" (1886-1894), opaque watercolor, Brooklyn Museum.

Heresies, 3.1.1. The identification is also made by Polycrates, Bishop of Ephesus, who is quoted by Eusebius in *Church History* 3.31.3 and 5.24.2-3.

of faithful friends huddled below is fascinating for all it implies.

First, Jesus addresses his mother not as "Mother," but as "woman," translated appropriately as "dear woman" by the NIV. We might sense a coldness in the term as used in our culture, but in Jesus' culture, it was perfectly proper for a man to address a woman this way – but still strange for a son to a mother.[6] The reason for this more formal address is probably that Jesus intends his words to be understood as a formal testamentary disposition under Jewish family law.[7]

As Mary's firstborn, Jesus is legally responsible for her welfare, to ensure that she has a place to live and food to eat during her widowhood. Jesus entrusts his mother to John's care instead and John takes this commission seriously:

> "From that time on, this disciple took her into his home."[8] (John 19:27b)

---

[6] Brown, *Death of the Messiah*, p. 1020. He notes that the word is not found elsewhere for a son addressing his mother (citing P. Benoit, *Jesus and the Gospel* (Herder, 1973), p. 86).

[7] Beasley-Murray, *John*, p. 349. We see somewhat similar formula-like language in the Book of Tobit, part of the Apocrypha that appears in Catholic, Orthodox, and Anglican Bibles. When Tobit is engaged to Sarah, Tobit is told: "Take your kinswoman; from now on you are her brother and she is your sister. She is given to you from today and forever" (Tobit 7:11, NRSV).

[8] While the bulk of church tradition considers Mary's grave to have been in the Valley of Kidron near Jerusalem some later sources write that she died in Ephesus where John was residing (Barnabas Meistermann, "Tomb of the Blessed Virgin Mary," *The Catholic Encyclopedia* (vol. 14; Robert Appleton Company, 1912)).

The Love of a Son for His Mother

Some see Jesus' Third Word as more than an act of filial devotion, but rather the Beloved Disciple (the Ideal Disciple) now joined to Mary (the new Eve). They picture Mary as being appointed as mother, not only of the Beloved Disciple, but of all disciples, hence of the Church.[9]

However, the text explains its meaning rather clearly: "From that time on, this disciple took her into his home" (John 19:27b). So the point of this verse is not that Mary is being appointed Mother of the Church. Rather, Jesus is clearly appointing John as responsible in his stead to care for his mother in her widowhood.

What Does This Word from the Cross Teach Us?

As I reflect on this Third Word from the Cross, I begin to see something about the extent of Jesus' love. Here he is: dying in agony, gasping for each breath. He sees his mother, the one who comforted him through all of childhood's cuts and bruises, teases and taunts. When he was a boy he would run home to mother and instantly be wrapped in her protective, comforting mother-love.

But now as he sees her at the foot of the cross, heartbroken, weeping, inconsolable, his heart goes out to her. Rather than being consumed by an

---

[9] Outlined by Brown, *Death of the Messiah,* pp. 1021-1022.

understandable concern for his own welfare, he is touched by hers.

She is a widow – soon to be a widow who will be known as mother to that crucified criminal, Jesus. Life will not be easy for her. The other children in the family (whether hers or Joseph's we just don't know) don't believe in him as she does (John 7:3-5). Though it might eventually be judged their legal duty to care for her, perhaps Jesus senses that such care would be less than what she deserves.[10]

What Are We to Learn from the Third Word?

What are we as Jesus' disciples to learn from this Word from the cross?

1. Love for our Family

First, we must love our parents – no matter what. Sometimes our parents misunderstand us or disapprove of decisions we make. Sometimes they can hurt

---

[10] Catholics and Orthodox disagree with Protestants on whether these named brothers and sisters (Matthew 13:55; Mark 6:3) are Joseph's children by a previous wife or Mary's other children. Origin (c. 185-254) wrote, "They [of Nazareth] thought, then, that He was the son of Joseph and Mary. But some say, basing it on a tradition in the Gospel according to Peter, as it is entitled, or 'The Book of James,' that the brethren of Jesus were sons of Joseph by a former wife, whom he married before Mary. Now those who say so wish to preserve the honor of Mary in virginity to the end, so that that body of hers which was appointed to minister to the Word which said, "The Holy Ghost shall come upon thee, and the power of the Most High shall overshadow thee," might not know intercourse with a man after that the Holy Ghost came into her and the power from on high overshadowed her" (Origin, *Commentary on Matthew*, 17).

us grievously. I can remember my dad's disapproval of me becoming a pastor in a "denominational" church and the pain I felt from that rejection. But I must love my dad.

Jesus, too, had felt the hurt of misunderstanding from his family – even his mother. It's apparent that during part of his ministry, at least, his family didn't understand him.

1. At the Wedding at Cana (John 2:1-11), Mary pushed Jesus to change the water into wine, even though he tells her, "My time has not yet come."

2. His family thought, "He is out of his mind," and went to take charge of him (Mark 3:21, 31-35) – his brothers apparently along with Mary.

3. "Even his own brothers did not believe in him." (John 7:5)

But whether they understand or even approve of us – whether we can even trust them at this point in our lives – we are told: "Honor your father and your mother" (Exodus 20:12). Christ-powered love can help heal the hurts from our families. We must love our parents.

2. Responsibility for our Family

Second, we are responsible for family obligations. Jesus was clear that his disciples must put commitment to him above family relationships – sometimes even using hyperbole to drive this point home.[11] Our obedience to Christ must become primary and obedience to parents must become secondary.

Having said that, just because we are Christians doesn't mean that we are absolved of family obligations. The Apostle Paul is adamant:

> "If anyone does not provide for his relatives, and especially for his immediate family, he has denied the faith and is worse than an unbeliever." (1 Timothy 5:8)

When we are immature believers, sometimes we take rash actions towards our families that in retrospect weren't filled with Christ's love. Our priorities, however, are clear: (1) God himself, (2) our families, (3) our work for God.

How do we reconcile our primary commitment to Jesus with responsibility for our families? Sometimes with great difficulty. But to put Christ first doesn't mean that we are free to neglect our other priorities – it means only that we get our priorities in proper relation to each other. God will give us wisdom to work this out.

Here at the end of his life, we see in Jesus the tender love of a son for his mother – a mother who had sometimes misunderstood him. As he dies, he settles his earthly obligations as best he can. We hear

---

[11] Matthew 10:37-38; Luke 14:26; Matthew 19:29; Mark 10:29-30; Luke 18:29-30; Mark 8:21-22.

him say, "Dear woman, here is your son ... Here is your mother" (John 19:26-27).

Prayer

Father, we see Jesus' example of love and responsibility. As wonderful and loving as family relationships can be, they are often complex and sometimes hurtful. We ask you to help us sort them out. Show us how to love you at the same time we love our family members. Give us the divine wisdom that we need so that we can love as Jesus loves. In His name, we pray. Amen.

Question for Personal Meditation

Q3. (John 19:26-27) Why does Jesus make St. John responsible for his mother Mary? What does this tell us about Jesus? How should we apply this in our own lives?
http://www.joyfulheart.com/forums/index.php?showtopic=881

Questions for Group Discussion

1. What do you think Mary is feeling while she is waiting at the cross for Jesus to die? What kinds of thoughts are going through her mind? (John 19:29-27)

2. Why, of all the disciples, do you think John is at the cross?

3. Why didn't Jesus make his brothers responsible for Mary? Why John?

4. What does this Third Word teach us about Jesus?

5. What are the implications of Jesus' Third Word for our own personal family relationships?

4. My God, My God, Why Have You Forsaken Me? (Mark 15:34)

"³³ At the sixth hour darkness came over the whole land until the ninth hour. ³⁴ And at the ninth hour Jesus cried out in a loud voice, *'Eloi, Eloi, lama sabachthani?'*–which means, 'My God, my God, why have you forsaken me?' ³⁵ When some of those standing

James J. Tissot, "My God, Why Hast Thou Forsaken Me?" (1886-1894), opaque watercolor, Brooklyn Museum.

near heard this, they said, 'Listen, he's calling Elijah.'" (Mark 15:33-35; also Matthew 27:45-47)

At the very center of the Seven Last Words, the Fourth Word is probably both Jesus' lowest point as well as a theological high point of the crucifixion. We'll spend a bit longer seeking to understand its implications.

The early crowds have long ago dispersed and the long time of waiting for death had begun. An eerie darkness has descended upon the entire area, a crushing gloom.

Six Hours on the Cross

The criminals on either side are still alive – and might have lived for days on the cross. But Jesus is not so strong. He has somehow endured a cruel scourging that would have killed lesser men. He has lost a lot of blood, even before climbing the hill to Golgotha and having his hands and feet nailed to the rough cross.

Mark tells us, "It was the third hour[1] when they crucified him" (Mark 15:25). Sometime after the crucifixion took place, Luke tells us: "It was now about the sixth hour, and darkness came over the

---

[1] Lane (*Mark*, p. 566-567) sees John's timing more credible than Mark's. Without any manuscript evidence Lane rejects Mark's "third hour" as probably "a gloss inserted by an early reviser." Others see more plausible an early trial with the crucifixion beginning around 9 a.m. and reaching a new phase between noon and 3 p.m. (France, *Matthew*, p. 1063, footnote 3).

whole land until the ninth hour" (Luke 23:44).[2] Jesus lasts only six hours.

Darkness over the Land

When darkness falls, something changes.

"It was now about the sixth hour, and darkness came over the whole land until the ninth hour, for the sun stopped shining...." (Luke 23:44-45a)

An African-American spiritual asks: "Were you there when the sun refused to shine?" Why the darkness? The word rendered "stopped shining" (NIV), "failed" (NRSV), "was darkened" (KJV) is *ekleipō* (from which we get our English word "eclipsed"). It means to "fail, give out, die out."[3]

An eclipse has taken place not so long ago on November 24, 29 AD, but what takes place this day is no natural eclipse. A normal eclipse would have been physically impossible during the time of the full moon on which Passover falls. We aren't told how it happens. The darkening may have been caused

[2] The Jews measured time from sunrise, approximately 6 am. John tells us that Jesus' trial before Pilate took place about the sixth hour (John 19:14). There have been various attempts to reconcile this with the times given in the Synoptic hours. Based on two examples, Brook Foss Westcott (The *Gospel According to St. John*), put forward the theory that Roman time was counted from midnight, rather than the Jewish calculation of the hours from sunrise. But there seems to be no strong evidence to support this claim. For a discussion see Morris, *John*, pp. 800-801, footnote 34.

[3] *Ekleipō*, BDAG 306. Luke's diction is standard for description of an eclipse in ancient Greek literature.

locally by a *hamsin* or sirocco wind.[4] We just don't know.

Throughout Jerusalem – and especially in this killing ground – the darkness is felt, heavy and foreboding. But what does the darkness mean? What is its significance? There are probably several possibilities and levels of meaning:

1. A symbol of moral darkness, "when darkness reigns" (Luke 22:53).[5]

2. A fulfillment of prophecy.

> **"The sun will be turned to darkness**
> and the moon to blood
> before the coming of the great and dreadful
>   day of the LORD." (Joel 2:31)

> "'In that day,' declares the Sovereign LORD,
> **'I will make the sun go down at noon**
> **and darken the earth in broad daylight.**
> I will turn your religious feasts into mourn-
> ing
> and all your singing into weeping.
> I will make all of you wear sackcloth
> and shave your heads.
> I will make that time like mourning
> for an only son
> and the end of it like a bitter day.'"
> (Amos 8:9-10)

---

[4] Marshall, *Luke*, p. 875.

[5] Darkness is a symbol of ignorance, spiritual blindness, and evil (for example, Luke 1:79; 11:34; and often in the Gospel of John).

3. A portent of the death of a king. Philo, a first century AD Jewish writer, saw supernatural eclipses as "indications either of the impending death of some king or of the destruction of some city."[6]

4. The Father's anger at how his only begotten Son is being treated:

> "The rising **sun will be darkened**
> and the moon will not give its light.
> I will punish the world for its evil,
> the wicked for their sins.
> I will put an end to
>   the arrogance of the haughty
> and will humble the pride of the ruthless."
> (Isaiah 13:10b-11)

5. The Father's judgment on the sins of the world being borne on Christ's shoulders as he hangs on the cross. This best fits my understanding of what was taking place at that time. The Lamb of God was bearing in himself the sins of the world!

A Darkness that Can Be Felt

The darkness was palpable, "a darkness that could be felt," reminiscent of the darkness over the land of Egypt in the Ninth Plague:

> "Then the LORD said to Moses, 'Stretch out your hand toward the sky so that darkness will spread over Egypt – darkness that can be

---

[6] Philo, *De Providentia* 2.50.

> felt.' So Moses stretched out his hand toward
> the sky, and **total darkness covered all Egypt
> for three days**." (Exodus 10:21-22)

I don't think the similarity between the three days
and the three hours is accidental.

Crying in a Loud Voice

Now in deep torment:

> "Jesus cried out in a loud voice" (Mark 15:34;
> Matthew 27:46)

Mark uses the verb *boaō* to describe this cry: "to
use one's voice at high volume, call, shout, cry out." It
can be used of emotionally charged cries of joy or of
excited crowds, but especially "of pleading petitions
or anguished outcries." [7] It is used of a man begging
Jesus to heal his son (Luke 9:38), of the desperate
blind man who will not be silenced, but cries, "Jesus,
Son of David, have mercy on me!" (Luke 18:38), and
of the shrieks of people as evil spirits leave them
(Acts 8:7). It is also used of the voice crying in the
wilderness: "Prepare the way of the Lord!" (Isaiah
40:3; Matthew 3:3, etc.).

---

[7] *Boaō*, BDAG 180, 1b. Matthew uses the related verb *anaboaō*, "cry out"
(BDAG 59). The word is also used of Elizabeth's prophetic cry upon
seeing Mary (Luke 1:42).

Eloi, Eloi, My God, My God!

In the Fourth Word from the cross, Jesus is quoting the first verse of Psalm 22, a psalm full of predictions of his crucifixion:

> "[34] And at the ninth hour Jesus cried out in a loud voice, *'Eloi,*[8] *Eloi, lama sabachthani?'*– which means, 'My God, my God, why have you forsaken me?' [35] When some of those standing near heard this, they said, 'Listen, he's calling Elijah.'" (Mark 15:34-35)

Some of those listening seem to have mistaken the call of "Eloi" with a call for Elijah.[9] In those days the Jews considered Elijah as one who would come in the Last Days to be a helper in time of need, to save the righteous.[10]

It is noteworthy that this is the only time that Jesus addresses "God" this way in prayer. In all his other recorded prayers he uses the term "Father," probably reflecting the intimate form *Abba*. But here in his hour of greatest desolation, he addresses God as would any other supplicant. This doesn't represent loss of faith. The fact that he is praying, "My God," shows

---

[8] In Mark, "Eloi" is formed from two Aramaic words, *El*, "God" + pronoun suffix "my." Brown (*Death*, pp. 1051-1058) provides a detailed analysis of the underlying language of this verse in Aramaic, Hebrew, and transliteration in Greek.

[9] "Elijah" would have been pronounced "'*Ēliyyâ*" or perhaps even "'*Ēli*" in a shortened version (S.C. Layton, *Zeitschrift für die alttestamentliche Wissenschaft* 108 (1996) 611-12, cited by France, Matthew, p. 1077, fn. 19).

[10] Joachim Jeremias, "*Hēl(e)ias*," TDNT 2:928-941.

that he still trusts God. But the intimacy of fellowship seems to have been broken. There is a loss of ontact.[11] Jesus can no longer feel his Father's presence.

Why Have You Forsaken Me?

"Forsaken" is a hard word for us to even think about. In Greek it is *enkataleipō*, "to separate connection with someone or something, forsake, abandon, desert."[12] We are so steeped in the promises from the Old and New Testaments to the contrary:[13]

> "I will never leave you or forsake you."
> (Hebrews 13:5, NRSV)

But clearly, Jesus senses that he is utterly forsaken by God.

Attempts to Mitigate the Cry of Desolation

Doesn't Jesus' forsakenness somehow suggest that he wasn't divine after all? How could Jesus as Son of God be separated from the Father? Isn't this an oxymoron?

Some have tried to lessen the incongruity by suggesting that by calling out the first words of Psalm 22 Jesus is calling attention to the entire psalm, which ends on an upswing of hope and triumph in verses 22-31.

---

[11] R.T. France says, "This shout expresses not a loss of faith, but a (temporary) loss of contact" (France, *Matthew*, p. 1077).

[12] *Enkataleipō*, BDAG 273, 2. The Hebrew equivalent in Psalm 22:1 is ʿāzab, "to depart, to abandon, and to loose" (Carl Schultz, ʿāzab, TWOT #1549).

[13] Joshua 1:5; Deuteronomy 31:6, 8; 1 Chronicles 28:20.

It is true that in ancient times before the Psalms were numbered, a particular psalm would be referred to by its first line. And much of Psalm 22 obviously pre-figures the elements of Jesus' crucifixion. But to suggest that by speaking the first verse of Psalm 22 Jesus was actually signaling the hope and triumph with which the Psalm ends twists the obvious meaning of Jesus' cry. [14]

The phrase "Jesus cried out in a loud voice" makes it clear that this is a very real prayer reflecting the agony of the Cup drunk to its very dregs on the cross.

> "My God, my God,
> why have you **forsaken** me?
> Why are you so far from saving me,
> so far from the words of my groaning?"
> (Psalm 22:1)

Why Is Jesus Cut Off from God?

The question, "Why is Jesus cut off from God?" reveals the quandary that we're in. It suggests a division in the Trinity itself – which is unthinkable! We have no theology to explain or describe it. But cut off, Jesus is. Why?

A verse from the Old Testament helps us understand:

---

[14] Lane says, "The sharp edge of this word must not be blunted. Jesus' cry of dereliction is the inevitable sequel to the horror which he had experienced in the Garden of Gethsemane" (*Mark*, p. 572).

"But your **iniquities have separated you
   from your God**;
your sins have hidden his face from you,
so that he will not hear." (Isaiah 59:2)

God is holy and righteous, so much so that unholy men are in danger if they try to draw close to him – "For the LORD your God is a consuming fire" (Deuteronomy 4:24; cf. Hebrews 12:29). We must keep our distance. Our sins and iniquities have caused a separation between us and God – a great gulf or chasm between us. The Hebrew verb is *bādal*, "divide, separate, sever."[15] That he has "hidden his face from you" (Isaiah 59:2b) means that we can't experience communion with him or sense his presence in our lives. "He will not hear" (Isaiah 59:2c).

The Lamb of God

But what does this have to do with the sinless Jesus? Paul explains:

"God made him who had no sin to **be sin for
us**, so that in him we might become the righteousness of God." (2 Corinthians 5:21)

Jesus is forsaken by God because he has taken our sins upon him. He is atoning for our sins. He is, "the **Lamb of God**, who **takes away the sin of the world**." (John 1:29). John is probably referring to Jesus as the

---

[15] Hiphil stem, Thomas E. McComisky, *bādal*, TWOT #203; BDB 95.

ultimate Paschal or Passover Lamb, a sacrifice made on behalf of the whole world (Exodus 12:1-13).[16]

The Garden of Gethsemane

Jesus' struggle to complete the Father's plan of redemption intensifies in the Garden of Gethsemane, the night before Jesus is crucified. Luke describes the scene:

> "[Jesus] withdrew about a stone's throw beyond [his disciples], knelt down and prayed, **'Father, if you are willing, take this cup from me; yet not my will, but yours be done.'** ... And being in anguish, he prayed more earnestly, and his sweat was like drops of blood falling to the ground." (Luke 22:41-42, 44)

The "cup" is used as a figurative expression for "destiny." Several times in the Bible we read of drinking a cup of suffering and judgment.[17] Jesus refers to drinking "the cup the Father has given me" (John 18:11; Matthew 20:22; 26:39; Mark 14:36).

Jesus' "cup," however, wasn't death, even death on the cross. His "cup" is the requirement that the holy Jesus bear our unholy sins and, as a result,

---

[16] You can learn more about the sacrifice for sin in my study *Behold, the Lamb of God* (2007), chapter 1, "The Lamb of God: Basic Concepts of Sacrifice."

[17] Isaiah 51:17, 22; Lamentations 4:21; Psalm 11:6; 75:8; Revelation 14:10; 16:19; 18:6.

receive in himself the judgment and punishment of God for our sins.

Jesus knows that the cross would mean separation from God. He struggles hard against it. Yet in the end, he prays, "Not my will, but yours be done" (Luke 22:42). He has made his decision.

The Darkness, the Horror, and the Forsakenness

Now the horror and magnitude of this "cup" come in full fury as the darkness of God's judgment grows heavy and he feels the Father's comforting presence sucked away. He who has been with the Father from all eternity is now utterly alone!

The Father's focus at this hour is severe judgment upon the sins Jesus is bearing.

Jesus' agonizing cry, "My God, My God, why have you forsaken me," enables us just a tiny glimpse of what it must have cost Jesus to die for our sins. Our forgiveness is not free, dear friends, neither for the Father nor for the Son. It wrenches them apart and puts them on opposite sides – as enemies – if only for a little while.

Jesus' agonizing saying from the cross teaches us something about how much the Father and Son both love us – so much that that they are willing to sever for a time their love for each other. Now, perhaps, we can understand better the Fourth Word from the cross:

"My God, my God, why have you forsaken me?" (Mark 15:34b)

A song springs forth in my consciousness, the chorus of a Charles Wesley hymn familiar from my youth:

"Amazing love! How can it be,
That Thou, my God, shouldst die for me?"[18]

Prayer

Father, Lord Jesus, how can we ever thank You enough. In the face of such determined and sacrificial love, our paltry and vacillating love seems so unworthy. Teach us, teach me, to love You as You love me. Help us to be both able and willing to understand the costliness of real love as You do. In your holy name we humbly come, kneel at your feet, and pray. Amen.

Question for Personal Meditation

Q4. (Mark 15:34) What does Jesus' Fourth Word from the cross teach us about faith? About commitment? About love? What effect should this understanding have on our lives?

http://www.joyfulheart.com/forums/index.php?showtopic=882

---

[18] "And Can It Be that I Should Gain?" words: Charles Wesley (1738), music: "Sagina," Thomas Campbell (1825). The full words and tune are available on HymnTime.com.

Questions for Group Discussion

1. How long was Jesus on the cross? In what way did the period seem to change about half-way through? (Mark 15:25, 33-34)

2. Why do you think the sun stopped shining? What did it signify? (Mark 15:33)

3. What does the loudness of Jesus' voice tell us about his mental and emotional states? (Mark 15:34)

4. What is the significance of Mark 15:34 including a quotation from Psalm 22?

5. In what sense was Jesus forsaken? Why must he be forsaken at this time? (Mark 15:34)

6. What was the "cup" that Jesus accepted in the Garden of Gethsemane? (Luke 22:41-44)

7. In what way does this Fourth Word reveal love? (Mark 15:34)

5. I Thirst (John 19:28)

It is near the end of Jesus' human life. He senses it. He has hung on the cross for six hours now.

It has become hard for Jesus to even get a breath. Hung from his arms, he must pull himself up each time he wants to breathe. His shoulders ache, his mouth is parched. He is exhausted.

The Roman soldier pushes a sponge on a reed up to Jesus' lips. James J. Tissot, "I Thirst" (1886-1894), opaque watercolor, Brooklyn Museum.

And yet he does not want to die without a final word. He asks for something to drink to wet his lips for this final effort.

"²⁸ Later, knowing that all was now completed, and so that the Scripture would be fulfilled, Jesus said, **"I am thirsty."** ²⁹ A jar of wine vinegar was there, so they soaked a sponge in it, put the sponge on a stalk of the hyssop plant, and lifted it to Jesus' lips." (John 19:28-29)

The Fulfillment of Scripture

"Knowing that all was now completed, and so that the Scripture would be fulfilled...." (John 19:28a)

What Scripture was fulfilled here? A Psalm of lamentation, written by David, seems to have been fulfilled literally in Jesus:

"They put **gall**[1] in my food
and **gave me vinegar**[2] **for my thirst**." (Psalm 69:21)

Apparently Jesus asked for something to quench his thirst in order to fulfill Psalm 69:21.

The First Offering of Wine

This was not the first time Jesus had been offered wine. Both Mark and Matthew observe that he was

---

[1] "Gall" (Hebrew rō'sh, Greek Septuagint cholē) probably refers to a Babylonian plant name which originally meant "head" of some kind of plant. It comes to mean "poison" and "poisonous" and occurs twelve times in the OT. In Psalm 69:21 it is used figuratively as "bitter herbs" (TWOT #2098).

[2] Vinegar (Hebrew ḥōmeṣ) comes from ḥāmēṣ, "be sour, be leavened" (TWOT #679b).

offered bitter wine just prior to being crucified (Matthew 27:34; Mark 15:23). Perhaps this was intended as an intoxicant for those about to suffer pain. A group of Jerusalem women, as an act of piety, provided for a condemned man a vessel of wine containing a grain of frankincense to numb him.[3] Jesus refuses to drink this. He has committed himself to the Father to offer himself as a sacrifice. To attempt to lessen the pain of this sacrifice would have somehow been going back on this commitment.

The Second Offering of Wine Vinegar (Posca)

The offering of something to quench his thirst after hanging on the cross for some time is a separate incident.

> "A jar of wine vinegar was there, so they soaked a sponge in it, put the sponge on a stalk of the hyssop plant, and lifted it to Jesus' lips." (John 19:29)

---

[3] "Again, what of Rabbi Hiyya ben Ashi's dictum in Rabbi Hisda's name: When one is led out to execution, he is given a goblet of wine containing a grain of frankincense, in order to benumb his senses, for it is written, Give strong drink unto him that is ready to perish, and wine unto the bitter in soul. And it has also been taught; The noble women in Jerusalem used to donate and bring it. If these did not donate it, who provided it? As for that, it is certainly logical that it should be provided out of the public [funds]: Since it is written. 'Give', [the implication is] of what is theirs" (Babylonian Talmud, *Sanhedrin* 43a). Mark mentions "wine mingled with myrrh" (Mark 15:23). First century army physician Dioscorides Pedanius observed the narcotic properties of myrrh (*Materia Medica* 1.64.3).

Wine vinegar (*oxos*) didn't have any alcohol left, but was sour wine that had turned to vinegar. Wine is made from grape juice. Yeast fermentation causes sugar to be transformed into alcohol, which continues until the alcohol content reaches about 11% to 12%. Wine vinegar, on the other hand, is made by the action of acetic acid bacteria on alcohol to produce acetic acid. Since the bacteria that cause this reaction are aerobic, they require that the wine be exposed to oxygen in order to form vinegar.

What is a container of wine vinegar doing on Golgotha that day? It is posca, a drink popular with soldiers of the Roman army, made by diluting sour wine vinegar with water. It was inexpensive, considered more thirst quenching than water alone, prevented scurvy, killed harmful bacteria in the water, and the vinegary taste made bad smelling water more palatable. All over the empire, posca was the soldier's drink of choice. The soldiers had brought posca to sustain them during their crucifixion duty. They weren't getting drunk on it, just using it to quench their own thirst.

The Sponge

While a condemned criminal might be able to drink wine prior to being crucified, drinking from a cup while hanging on the cross wasn't practical. So when Jesus indicated his thirst, the soldiers used a sponge to give him posca to slake his thirst.

What was a sponge (Greek *sponges*) doing on Golgotha that day? It seems scarcely the thing you'd expect to find. Again, sponges were part of a Roman soldier's kit. Sponges were found along the Mediterranean coast, were widely used in ancient times to line and pad a soldier's helmet. Soldiers also used sponges as drinking vessels.[4]

No doubt one of the soldiers offered Jesus a drink of posca from his own supply, using his own sponge. A soldier wasn't required to share his drink with the criminals under his care. But he had seen that Jesus was dying unlike any other criminal he had ever seen. No cursing, no blaming, no anger.

A Man Like No Other

What was it like to watch Jesus' slow death? Perhaps it had impressed the soldier with something like St. Peter's words:

> "'He committed no sin,
> and no deceit was found in his mouth.'
> When they hurled their insults at him,
> he did not retaliate;
> when he suffered, he made no threats.
> Instead, he entrusted himself
> to him who judges justly." (1 Peter 2:22-23)

St. Peter concludes this passage with something, however, that the soldier did not yet know, echoing

---

[4] Thomas F. Johnson, "Sponge," ISBE 4:605. Sponges were also carried by Roman soldiers to use the way we use toilet paper.

the words of the Suffering Servant passage of Isaiah 53:

> "He himself bore our sins in his body on the tree, so that we might die to sins and live for righteousness; by his wounds you have been healed." (1 Peter 2:24)

The posca offered by a soldier on his sponge that day was an act of mercy to the One who was bringing God's mercy to all humankind.

The Hyssop

> "They ... put the sponge on a stalk of the hyssop plant, and lifted it to Jesus' lips." (John 19:29)

John makes a point of specifying the hyssop plant, a small bush with blue flowers and highly aromatic leaves,[5] whereas the Synoptic Gospels refer to it as a "stick" (NIV, NRSV) or "reed" (KJV, RSV).[6] What is the significance of hyssop? Hyssop was used to sprinkle blood on the doorposts and lintels on the first Passover (Exodus 12:22). It was associated with purification and sacrifices in the tabernacle (Leviticus

---

[5] *Hyssōpos*, BDAG 104.

[6] *Kalamos*, "1. reed, 2. stalk, staff" (BDAG 502; Matthew 27:48; Mark 15:36). This sometimes causes confusion, our dramatic depictions of the cross usually picture Jesus elevated far above the onlookers. However, most likely his cross was much shorter. All that was necessary was to have the feet elevated high enough so they didn't touch the ground. We have some reports of the feet of crucified criminals being ravaged by dogs. A common guess is that Jesus' cross stood some 7 feet high (Brown, *Death*, pp. 948-949).

14:4, 6; Numbers 19:6, 18). No doubt John had this in mind when he wrote his Gospel.

Receiving the Posca

John tells us that Jesus actually drank some of the vinegary posca from the sponge.[7]

> "When he had received the drink, Jesus said, 'It is finished.' With that, he bowed his head and gave up his spirit." (John 19:30)

For a few seconds, at least, Jesus sucked the posca from the sponge. He didn't drink long enough to slake what must have been moderate to severe dehydration from loss of blood, exposure to the elements, and the necessity of gasping for breath through his mouth.

The end was near. So he drank only enough to moisten his parched throat so that his last words of triumph might be heard across the hilltop of Golgotha.

What Does This Word Tell Us?

What does the Fifth Word say to us? I see three things that this Word reminds us of:

1. Jesus' Physical Humanity

First and probably of greatest importance, Jesus' word "I thirst," reminds us of Jesus' physical nature, his humanity.

---

[7] "Received" (*lambanō*) carries the idea "to take into one's possession, take, acquire" (BDAG 583, 3).

This was no play-acting on the cross – a divine being pretending to undergo a physical act of torture that could not touch him. This was tangible physical suffering, of which extreme thirst is the one element most of us can readily identify with from our own personal experience.

There was a heresy afoot in the Hellenistic world that Jesus didn't really come in flesh and blood, much less die a gruesome physical death on the cross. Flesh was of the evil realm, they believed, and could never be holy. Only spirit was capable of the divine. So Jesus didn't really die, he only appeared to. He was only pretending. Thus said Docetism and Gnosticism.

The Apostle John was combating an early form of this heresy in his letters:

> "... Every spirit that confesses that Jesus Christ has come in the flesh is from God, and every spirit that does not confess Jesus is not from God. And this is the spirit of the antichrist...." (1 John 4:2-3)

> "Many deceivers, who do not acknowledge Jesus Christ as coming in the flesh, have gone out into the world. Any such person is the deceiver and the antichrist." (2 John 7)

Jesus Fifth Word, "I thirst," reminds us that Jesus died *in the flesh* for us and for our sins.

2. Jesus' Awareness of Scripture

Second, "I thirst" reminds us of Jesus' extensive knowledge of the prophetic scriptures concerning his suffering and death – and his willingness to fulfill each of them to the letter. The best known passage, of course, is the Servant Song from Isaiah 53:

> "He poured out his life unto death,
> and was numbered with the transgressors.
> For he bore the sin of many,
> and made intercession for the transgressors."
> (Isaiah 53:12)

He knew it well and referred to it again and again.[8] Jesus' action to ask for a drink is deliberately prompted by his knowledge of Scripture and determination to fulfill it:

> "... So that the Scripture would be fulfilled,
> Jesus said, 'I am thirsty.'" (John 19:28)

3. Jesus' Determination to Complete His Task

Third, Jesus said, "I thirst" to strengthen himself and ease his throat so that he might cry out his final words from the cross "with a loud voice." He was summoning himself to bring it all to completion.

Prayer

Father, extreme thirst, being parched, is something I can relate to. But adding to the physical torment and

[8] See my "Quotations, References and Allusions in the New Testament to Isaiah 53 and other Servant Songs," as part of the Behold, the Lamb of God Bible Study. www.jesuswalk.com/lamb/isaiah53_nt_allusions.htm

exhaustion was the crushing spiritual aloneness. That is beyond my experience. Thank you for your love that conquered all to save us. In Jesus' name, I pray. Amen.

Question for Personal Meditation

Q5. (John 19:28) What do you learn from Jesus' Fifth Word: "I thirst"? What does this tell us about Jesus? What does this tell us about his experience on the cross?

http://www.joyfulheart.com/forums/index.php?showtopic=883

Questions for Group Discussion

1. What are the reasons that Jesus would have been thirsty? Physiologically, what would have been going on in a person suffering as Jesus did?

2. What Scriptures are fulfilled by John 19:28-30 or may refer to this aspect of the crucifixion? Why was fulfilling Scripture important to Jesus?

3. What is the significance of the sponge being offered to Jesus on a branch of hyssop? (John 19:29)

4. Why do you think the New Testament makes such a strong point about Jesus' physical suffering? What difference would it make if Jesus were a divine person who didn't actually suffer on the cross? What difference would it make if Jesus were only a human being martyred on the cross?

6. It Is Finished (John 19:30)

"When he had re-
ceived the drink, Jesus
said, **'It is finished.'**
With that, he bowed his
head and gave up his
spirit." (John 19:30)

Jesus' journey had
begun in a simple stable
in the City of David
thirty some years before.
Now it was finished.

What Did Jesus Come to Accomplish?

What was finished?
What was this mission
that was now finished?
Why did Jesus come?
Let's look at how Jesus
defined his mission – and later, how his apostles
understood it. We read about his commission to

A remarkable watercolor by James
J. Tissot, "It is finished!
Consummatum est!" (1886-1894)
showing the crucified but
triumphant Christ, behind him the
holy name of Yahweh in Hebrew
letters, and surrounded by the
prophets holding up their scrolls of
prophecy which he has fulfilled.
(Brooklyn Museum, NYC).

"preach the Gospel to the poor" (Luke 4:18, 43), "to bring life" (John 10:10b), "to destroy the devil's work" (1 John 3:8b), "to bring fire upon the earth," (Luke 12:49), and "to testify to the truth" (John 18:37). But each of these seems like a means or aspect of the ultimate purpose, to save us from our sins. Consider these purpose statement verses:

> "Look, the Lamb of God, who **takes away the sin** of the world!" (John 1:29)

> "For the Son of Man came to seek and to **save** what was lost." (Luke 19:10)

> "For even the Son of Man did not come to be served, but to serve, and to **give his life as a ransom** for many." (Mark 10:45)

> "Christ Jesus came into the world to **save sinners**." (1 Timothy 1:15)

> "But you know that he appeared so that he might **take away our sins**." (1 John 3:5)

The Cup and the Baptism

Jesus had a very clear view of what lay ahead of him. He used two metaphors: "To drink the cup," to partake fully of an event, and "to be baptized," to be immersed fully in the event.

> "Can you **drink the cup** I drink or **be baptized** with the baptism I am baptized with?" (Mark 10:38)

> "But I have a **baptism** to undergo, and how distressed I am until it is completed! (Luke 12:50)

> "Father, if you are willing, take this **cup** from me; yet not my will, but yours be done." (Luke 22:42)

> "Jesus commanded Peter, 'Put your sword away! Shall I not **drink the cup** the Father has given me?'" (John 18:11)

The cross in all its horror – and in its redemptive power to bear the sins of the world – hung heavily on Jesus during his last days in the flesh. His struggle in the Garden of Gethsemane was the climax, the point at which he surrendered ultimately to the Father's will. And now the cup had been drunk, the baptism completed. It is finished.

It Is Finished!

Look again at the passage. It is remarkable in how it repeats one singular idea – completion, fulfillment, finishing.

> "Later, knowing that all was now **completed** (*teleō*), and so that the Scripture would be **fulfilled** (*teleioō*), Jesus said, 'I am thirsty' ... When he had received the drink, Jesus said, '**It is finished** (*teleō*).' With that, he bowed his head and gave up his spirit." (John 19:28, 30)

These three words derive from the same Greek root, *telos*, which means "end" – primarily a termination point, then by extension, the end to which all things relate, the aim, the purpose.[1]

"Completed / finished / accomplished" in verses 28 and 30 is the related verb *teleō*, "to complete an activity or process, bring to an end, finish, complete something." With regard to time, it means, "come to an end, be over."[2] Moreover the tense of this verb is important to us – perfect tense (*tetelestai*). In Greek the perfect tense signifies a past action, the effect of which continues into the present. It has been completed and is still complete. The effect of the tense in this verb is a sense of finality.

In the last couple of centuries, scholars have found thousands of papyrus scraps with Greek writing on them. Many of these are mundane commercial documents in which we find this word. Moulton and Milligan pored over many of these receipts and contracts to better understand New Testament Greek. They observed that receipts are often introduced by the phrase *tetelestai*, usually written in an abbreviated manner indicating that the bill had been paid in full.[3] The obligation has been completed. The debt has been paid off. *Tetelestai* – it is finished.

---

[1] *Telos*, Thayer.

[2] *Teleō*, BDAG 997, 1.

[3] J.H. Moulton and G. Milligan, *Vocabulary of the Greek Text: Illustrated edition the Papyri and Other Non-Literary Sources* (Eerdmans, 1957), p. 630, under *teleō*.

A Cry of Victory

It is clear from Matthew and Mark that just before Jesus breathed his last, he "cried out again in a loud voice" (Matthew 27:50, cf. Mark 15:37). John gives us the content of this loud cry: "It is finished!"

Those who are defeated go out with a whimper, but the victor announces his victory loudly and broadly: "It is finished!" The victory shout of Jesus echoed across the small flat hilltop and to the world beyond. It is finished!

The Announcement of Obedience Fulfilled

It is a cry of accomplishment, but it is also an announcement of obedience fulfilled. This shout began in the painful will of the Father – the cup, the baptism, the suffering, the cross. "It is finished" announces the full obedience of the One who, though equal with God:

> "... Made himself nothing,
> taking the very nature of a servant,
> being made in human likeness.
> And being found in appearance as a man,
> he humbled himself
> and became obedient to death
> – even death on a cross!

> Therefore God exalted him
>   to the highest place
> and gave him the name
> that is above every name,
> that at the name of Jesus
> every knee should bow,
> in heaven and on earth and under the earth,
> and every tongue confess
> that Jesus Christ is Lord,
> to the glory of God the Father."
> (Philippians 2:7-11)

Make no mistake. The ability to say, "It is finished" to the Father's commission was not the beginning of some kind of "glory road," but the end. It was the final culmination of a life of obedience, humility, and suffering that now ushers in a new era.

What Should We Learn from "It Is Finished"?

When we meditate on this Sixth Word from the cross, what should we learn for our lives? This is what I see.

1. We Are to Live Lives of Purpose

First, we are to live lives of purpose. Unless Jesus had a purpose, a mission to complete, the words, "It is finished" would have had little meaning. He wasn't speaking of his earthly life that was finished – in fact, his life has no beginning and has no end.

Rather, he is speaking of that which the Father had instructed him to do.

Our lives may not be so clear, so purpose-driven as Jesus' life. However, I believe that one of the signs of maturity in our lives is to discern our spiritual gifts and abilities, and then order our lives so as to maximize what God has given.

Jesus told the Parables of the Talents (Matthew 25:14-30) and the Pounds (Luke 19:11-27). In each case, success for the servant was to "trade with" what the master had given him in order to produce the largest possible outcome for the master, given each servant's unique talents, time, and circumstances. The reward was to hear the master say, "Well done, good and faithful servant ... enter into the joy of your master" (Matthew 25:21, RSV).

2. We Are to Live Lives of Focus

Second, living lives of purpose requires us to focus on our priorities. Instead of living scatter-shot lives, we are to be marksmen that aim carefully at the target and make our shots count. This requires focus and discipline. It means saying "No" to some choices so that we can say "Yes" to opportunities that are even better.

3. We Are to Live Lives of Obedience

Third, to be able to say, "It is finished," as Jesus did, our lives must be marked by obedience. Jesus is God, but in his earthly life he willingly obeyed. "He humbled himself and became obedient to death" (Philippians 2:8). Paul put it this way:

> "I have been crucified with Christ and I no longer live, but Christ lives in me. The life I live in the body, I live by faith in the Son of God, who loved me and gave himself for me." (Galatians 2:20)

Obedience is the opposite of independent action. It means living in obedience to God, not to ourselves.

4. We Must Be Willing to Suffer to Achieve God's Purpose

Finally, to say "It is finished," we must be willing to suffer to achieve God's purpose for our lives. We continue in the sunny summer days as well as the stormy winters of our lives. We don't give up just because things are difficult. We are willing to suffer whatever is necessary to complete the Father's plan for our lives.

When our lives are over, we want to be able to say with St. Paul,

> "The time of my departure has come. I have fought the good fight, I have finished the race, I have kept the faith. From now on there is reserved for me the crown of righteousness, which the Lord, the righteous judge, will give me on that day, and not only to me but also to all who have longed for his appearing." (2 Timothy 4:6-8)

And with Jesus to say: "It is finished!"

Prayer

Father, I've wasted much of the momentum of my life because I've tried to go in so many directions. Please corral me so that I will focus on your purposes and your direction for me, that I might finish this life well. In Jesus' name, I pray. Amen.

Question for Personal Meditation

Q6. (John 19:30) What had Jesus "finished"? What can we learn for our own lives from this Sixth Word: "It is finished"?

http://www.joyfulheart.com/forums/index.php?showtopic=884

Questions for Group Discussion

1. What did Jesus come to accomplish? What was his "prime directive"?
2. What was the "cup," the "baptism" that he faced in order to accomplish his mission?
3. What was the significance of the word "Finished" written on ancient papyrus receipts?
4. Why did Jesus shout out this Sixth Word, rather than say it quietly? (John 19:30)
5. What do we learn from the Sixth Word about purpose? About focus? About obedience? (John 19:30)
6. How is the willingness to suffer vital to finishing one's mission?

7. Father, Into Your Hands I Commit My Spirit (Luke 23:46)

"⁴⁴ It was now about the sixth hour, and darkness came over the whole land until the ninth hour, ⁴⁵ for the sun stopped shining. And the curtain of the temple was torn in two. ⁴⁶ Jesus called out with a loud voice, 'Father, into your hands I commit my spirit.' When he had said this, he breathed his last." (Luke 23:44-46)

James J. Tissot, "The Death of Christ" (1886-1894), opaque watercolor, Brooklyn Museum.

Under the Romans, crucifixion was often a long, drawn-out process. That was the idea – a prolonged, tortuous death for criminals would not only inspire horror in the hearts of the populace, but also provide a public reminder of the danger of any attempt to resist Roman power.

Criminals would often last for days before they finally succumbed, though on this day, the day before a Sabbath, any surviving criminals would be killed by breaking their legs (John 19:31-33) and their bodies removed from the cross through some kind of agreement brokered with the chief priests so as not to overly offend Jewish sensibilities.

Temple Curtain Torn

It was a time of ominous signs in the heavens and on the earth beneath.

> "[44] It was now about the sixth hour, and darkness came over the whole land until the ninth hour, [45] for the sun stopped shining. And the curtain of the temple was torn[1] in two." (Luke 23:44-45)

We discussed the eerie darkness under the Fourth Word above. But in addition to the sun not shining, the curtain of the temple was rent.

---

[1] The word "torn" (NIV, NRSV), "rent" (KJV) is *schizō* (from which we get our English words "schism" and "schizophrenia"). Here it means "to divide by use of force, split, divide, separate, tear apart" (BDAG 981, 1b).

The curtain mentioned is the inner curtain that separates the Holy of Holies from the Holy Place.[2] Edersheim tells us that it consisted of two curtains that were 60 feet long and 30 feet wide, as thick as the palm of a man's hand, woven in 72 separate squares, and joined together.[3] Think of the force that would have been required to tear this massive curtain! Perhaps the earthquake caused the fall of a lintel to begin the vertical rip that went from top to bottom (Mark 15:38).[4]

But what does the rent curtain mean? The Gospel writers don't tell us. But it probably signifies: (1) an opening of the way between people and the very presence of God, brought about by Christ's redemption on the cross, or (2) a forewarning of the obsolescence and final destruction of the temple. Perhaps it means both of these.

---

[2] *Katapetasma*, BDAG 524. See also Hebrews 6:19 and 10:20.

[3] Edersheim writes, "That some great catastrophe, betokening the impending destruction of the Temple, had occurred in the Sanctuary about this very time, is confirmed by not less than four mutually independent testimonies: those of Tacitus, of Josephus, of the Talmud, and of earliest Christian tradition" (*Life and Times*, 2:611). He cites *Yoma* 54a, *Kethub* 106a; *Sheqal*. viii. 5.

[4] Edersheim, *Life and Times*, 2:610. He cites Tacitus, *Hist.* v. 13; Josephus, *Wars* 6, 5, 3; *Jer. Yoma* 43c; *Yoma* 39b. Marshall, *Luke*, p. 874 notes Jewish references to such portents 40 years before the fall of Jerusalem, and cites Strack and Billerback I, 1045f., but notes that Josephus dates these in 66 AD. Edersheim (2:610) observes, "So in the Gospel according to the Hebrews, from which St. Jerome quotes (in Matthew 27:51, and in a letter of *Hedibia*) to the effect that the huge lintel of the Temple was broken and splintered, and fell. St. Jerome connects the rending of the Veil with this, and it would seem an obvious inference to connect again this breaking of the lintel with an earthquake."

Jesus Final Word (Luke 23:46)

> "Jesus called out with a loud voice,
> 'Father, into your hands I commit
> my spirit.' When he had said this,
> he breathed his last." (Luke 23:46)

These words are from a Psalm written by David:

> **"Into your hands I commit my spirit**;
> redeem me, O LORD, the God of truth."
> (Psalm 31:5)

They are part of an evening prayer used daily by devout Jews.[5]

Notice the loud voice – scarcely what one would expect from a man about to die. But Jesus seems determined that his final words be heard. His words are firm and confident. Let's examine three aspects of this Seventh Word.

1. A Word of Intimacy

First, Jesus speaks to God with intimacy. His time of desolation expressed by the Fourth Word is past. He prays to the Father as he has done throughout his ministry. For Jesus, death is no out-of-control enemy. No matter how bleak the moment, he knows his Father is present with him – now present to receive his spirit.

---

[5] Marshall, *Luke*, p. 876.

2. A Word of Trust

Second, Jesus entrusts himself to his Father. In Psalm 31:5 the word "commit" is the Hebrew verb *pāqad*. In our verse it occurs in the Hiphil stem, with the meaning "commit, entrust."[6] The corresponding Greek verb is *paratithēmi*, meaning, "to entrust to someone for safekeeping, give over, entrust, commend," particularly, "to entrust someone to the care and protection of someone."[7] As he lets go of this life, Jesus trusts his eternal destiny to the Father's everlasting arms.

3. A Word of Surrender

Finally, Jesus speaks a word of surrender. He gives up his human life to his Father who gave it to him 33 years before. The word "spirit" is the common word *pneuma*, "breathing, breath of life." It can refer to the Holy Spirit, but here refers to the personal spirit of Jesus, part of the human personality (Hebrews 4:12; 1 Thessalonians 5:23).[8]

Jesus prays his final prayer with this kind of equanimity and peace because he knows the Father, and knows that there is life with the Father beyond death. As a devout Jew he has prayed these words as part of

---

[6] *Pāqad*, BDG 823, H2a. The basic meaning of the word is "attend to, visit, muster, appoint." A similar idea is found in 1 Kings 14:27, where the king entrusts bronze shields to the commanders of the palace guard (1 Kings 14:27).

[7] *Paratithēmi*, BDAG 772, 3b. We see similar expressions in Acts 7:59 and 1 Peter 4:19.

[8] *Pneuma*, BDAG 832-836.

an evening prayer all his life. Now at the end of his life he prays them one last time – and lets go of human life[9] in order to embrace the Life that the Father has to offer in his own presence.

We pray, with Jesus, "Father, into your hands I commit my spirit"

Prayer

Father, when it comes time for us to let go of this life, help us do it with the same kind of faith and confidence that we see in Jesus. We love you, Lord. Thank you for our salvation and eternal life. In Jesus' name, we pray. Amen.

Question for Personal Meditation

Q7. (Luke 23:46) What does Jesus mean when he says, "Father, into your hands I commit my spirit"? Why does this saying comfort us so much?
http://www.joyfulheart.com/forums/index.php?showtopic=885

---

[9] The phrase "breathed his last" (NIV, NRSV), "gave up the ghost" (KJV) translates a verb from the same root as *pneuma*: *ekpneō*, "breathe out one's life/soul, expire," a euphemism for "die" (BDAG 308). See also Eduard Schweitzer, *"ekpneō,"* TDNT 6:452-453.

Questions for Group Discussion

1. What is the meaning of the curtain of the temple being torn in two? (Luke 23:45b)

2. What does Jesus mean when he says, "Father, into your hands I commit my spirit" (Luke 23:46)? Why does this saying comfort us so much?

3. What would you have felt like had you witnessed Jesus' crucifixion – if you didn't know the next chapter in the story?

4. Why is faith so important during the dark chapters of our lives? What does it take to shake off the numbness and depression and take hold of that faith once more?

Appendix 1. Questions for Group Discussion

You may reprint these questions at no cost to encourage participation and discussion in a group or service that is meditating on the Seven Last Words. For 8-1/2 x 11 question sheets, see:

www.jesuswalk.com/7-last-words/7-last-words-questions.pdf

To reprint the entire study, you can purchase reprint licenses at:

www.jesuswalk.com/books/7-last-words.htm

1. Father, Forgive Them (Luke 23:34)

1. What term do you usually use to address God? Why? How might your faith be affected if you started addressing God in your prayers as "Father"? How would it help you better understand the relationship between you and God?

2. In what sense can your sin be seen as a debt owed to God? How do you pay off a debt like that? On what just basis can God forgive this debt of sin?

3. What does knowledge of sin have to do with Jesus' forgiveness? At what level did Jesus' killers understand what they were doing?

4. Who was most responsible for killing Jesus? What responsibility do we bear for Jesus' death on the cross?

2. This Day You Will Be with Me in Paradise (Luke 23:43)

1. Why do you think one of the criminals on the cross insulted and mocked Jesus? What human trait prompted him to do this? (Luke 23:39)

2. Why does the other criminal rebuke him for his insults? On what grounds does he try to stop him? (Luke 23:40-41)

3. What did the thief have to believe about Jesus to cause him to ask him, "Jesus, remember me when you come into your kingdom" (Luke 23:42). What are the elements of his faith?

4. Did the thief confess his sins? Was he repentant?

5. How do you think the thief's request make Jesus feel?

6. What are the elements of Jesus' promise to the thief in Luke 23:43?

7. What are we disciples supposed to learn from this strange exchange on the crosses above our

heads? What does Jesus intend for us for to get out of this?

3. Woman, Behold Your Son (John 19:26-27)

1. What do you think Mary is feeling while she is waiting at the cross for Jesus to die? What kinds of thoughts are going through her mind? (John 19:29-27)
2. Why, of all the disciples, do you think John is at the cross?
3. Why didn't Jesus make his brothers responsible for Mary? Why John?
4. What does this Third Word teach us about Jesus?
5. What are the implications of Jesus' Third Word for our own personal family relationships?

4. My God, My God, Why Have You Forsaken Me? (Mark 15:34)

1. How long was Jesus on the cross? In what way did the period seem to change about halfway through? (Mark 15:25, 33-34)
2. Why do you think the sun stopped shining? What did it signify? (Mark 15:33)
3. What does the loudness of Jesus' voice tell us about his mental and emotional states? (Mark 15:34)

4. What is the significance of Mark 15:34 including a quotation from Psalm 22?

5. In what sense was Jesus forsaken? Why must he be forsaken at this time? (Mark 15:34)

6. What was the "cup" that Jesus accepted in the Garden of Gethsemane? (Luke 22:41-44)

7. In what way does this Fourth Word reveal love? (Mark 15:34)

5. I Thirst (John 19:28)

1. What are the reasons that Jesus would have been thirsty? Physiologically, what would have been going on in a person suffering as Jesus did?

2. What Scriptures are fulfilled by John 19:28-30 or may refer to this aspect of the crucifixion? Why was fulfilling Scripture important to Jesus?

3. What is the significance of the sponge being offered to Jesus on a branch of hyssop? (John 19:29)

4. Why do you think the New Testament makes such a strong point about Jesus' physical suffering? What difference would it make if Jesus were a divine person who didn't actually suffer on the cross? What difference would it make if Jesus were only a human being martyred on the cross?

6. It Is Finished (John 19:30)

1. What did Jesus come to accomplish? What was his "prime directive"?
2. What was the "cup," the "baptism" that he faced in order to accomplish his mission?
3. What was the significance of the word "Finished" written on ancient papyrus receipts?
4. Why did Jesus shout out this Sixth Word, rather than say it quietly? (John 19:30)
5. What do we learn from the Sixth Word about purpose? About focus? About obedience? (John 19:30)
6. How is the willingness to suffer vital to finishing one's mission?

7. Father, Into Your Hands I Commit My Spirit (Luke 23:46)

1. What is the meaning of the curtain of the temple being torn in two? (Luke 23:45b)
2. What does Jesus mean when he says, "Father, into your hands I commit my spirit" (Luke 23:46)? Why does this saying comfort us so much?
3. What would you have felt like had you witnessed Jesus' crucifixion – if you didn't know the next chapter in the story?

4. Why is faith so important during the dark chapters of our lives? What does it take to shake off the numbness and depression and take hold of that faith once more?

Appendix 2. Hymns and Songs Appropriate for Good Friday or Maundy Thursday Services

Here's a selection of some favorite songs, both old and new, that could be used in a Maundy Thursday or Good Friday service to commemorate the death of Christ for our sins. I'm sure it isn't complete. If you have suggestions for additional songs, please contact me.

Traditional

Most of these songs can be found with melodies at the CyberHymnal (www.hymntime.com/tch/)

"Alas! and Did My Savior Bleed," words: Isaac Watts (1707); music: "Martyrdom" (without the refrain), Hugh Wilson (1800); with the refrain "**At the Cross** ... where I first saw the light," Ralph E. Hudson (1885).

"At Calvary" ("Years I spent in vanity and pride..."), words: William R. Newell (1895), music: Daniel B. Towner (1895)

"And Can It Be that I Should Gain?" words: Charles Wesley (1738), Music: "Sagina," Thomas Campbell (1825)

"Are You Washed in the Blood?" words and music: Elisha A. Hoffman (1878)

"Beneath the Cross of Jesus," words: Elizabeth C. Celphane (1868), music: "St. Christopher," Frederick C. Maker (1881)

"Blessed Redeemer" ("Up Calvary's mountain..."), words: Avis m. Christiansen (1920), music: Harry D. Loes

"Calvary Covers It All," Words and Music by Mrs. Walter G. Taylor (© 1934, renewed 1962, The Rodeheaver Co.)

"Come to Calvary's Holy Mountain," words: James Montgomery (1819), music: "Consolation," Ludvig M. Lindeman (1871)

"Come Ye Sinners, Poor and Needy," words: Joseph Hart (1759), music: "Restoration," William Walker (1835)

"Down at the Cross" ("Glory to His Name"), words: Elisha A. Hoffman (1878), music: John H. Stockton (1878)

"Go to Dark Gethsemane," words: James Montgomery (1820), music: "Redhead," Richard Redhead (1853)

"Hallelujah! What a Savior," words and music: Philip P. Bliss (1875)

"I Know a Fount," words and music by Oliver Cooke (20th century)

"I Saw One Hanging on a Tree," words: John Newton (1779), music: Edwin O. Excell (1917)

"I Stand Amazed in the Presence of Jesus the Nazarene," words and music by Charles H. Gabriel (1905)

"In the Cross of Christ I Glory," words: John Bowring (1825), music: Ithamar D. Conkey (1849)

"In the Hour of Trial," words: James Montgomery (1834), music: "Penitence," Spencer Lane (1874)

"Jesus Walked this Lonesome Valley," words and music: African-American spiritual

"Jesus Paid It All" ("I heard the Savior say..."), words: Elivina M. Hall (1865), music: John T. Grape

"Jesus, Priceless Treasure," words: Johann Frank (1653), translated from German by Catherine Winkworth (1863), music: "Jesu Meine Fruede," Johann Sebastian Bach (1723)

"Jesus, the Son of God" ("Do you know Jesus...," "O sweet wonder ..."), words and music: Garfield T. Haywood (c. 1914)

"Jesus, Thy Blood and Righteousness," words: Nikolaus L. von Zinzendorf (1739), translated from German by John Wesley (1740), music: "Germany," William Gardiner (1815)

"Just As I Am," words: Charlotte Elliott, music: William Batchelder Bradbury

"Lead Me to Calvary" ("Lest I forget Gethsemane..."), words: Jennie E. Hussey, music: William J. Kirkpatrick

"Nothing but the Blood" ("What can wash away my sin?..."), words and music: Robert Lowry (1876)

"O Sacred Head Now Wounded," words: attributed to St. Bernard of Clairvaux (1153), translated from Latin by James W. Alexander (1830), music: "Passion Chorale," Hans L. Hassler (1601), harmony by Johann Sebastian Bach (1729)

"Rock of Ages, Cleft for Me," words: Augustus M. Toplady (1776), music: "Toplady," Thomas Hastings (1830)

"Savior, Thy Dying Love," words: Sylvanus D. Phelps (1862), music: "Something for Jesus," Robert Lowry (1871)

"The Old Rugged Cross" ("On a hill far away..."), words and music: George Bennard (1913)

"There Is a Green Hill Far Away," words: Cecil F. Alexander (1847), music: "Green Hill," Georg C. Stebbins

"There Is a Fountain Filled with Blood," words: William Cowper (1772), music: "Cleansing Fountain," 19th century American camp meeting tune

"'Tis Midnight, and on Olive's Brow," words: William B. Tappan, music: "Olive's Brow," William B. Bradbury (1853)

"Where You There?" words and music: African-American spiritual

"What Wondrous Love Is This?" words: attributed to Alexander Means, music: William Walker (1835)

"When I Survey the Wondrous Cross," words: Isaac Watts (1707), music: "Hamburg," Lowell Mason (1824)

"Wounded for Me," words: William G. J. Ovens (1869-1945) and Gladys Westcott Roberts, music: William G. J. Ovens

Contemporary

Words to most of these songs (and a portion of the tune) can be found in the fee-based Song Select service at CCLI.

"Amazing Love, O What Sacrifice," words and music by Graham Kendrick (© 1989, Make Way Music)

"Behold the Lamb," words and music: Dottie Rambo (© 1979, John T. Benson Publishing)

"Blessed Are the Broken," words and music by David Baroni (© 1994, Integrity's Praise! Music)

"Calvary" ("Jesus, I remember the cross"), words and music: Mike Nikkerud (© 2007, Planet Shakers Ministries)

"Crown of Thorns," words and music by Rick Stokes (© 1995, Rick Stokes)

"Forever My Love" ("The Nails in Your Hands"), words and music: Richard Cimino (© 1995, Richard Cimino)

"Fraction Anthem" ("Your body was broken for us..."), words and music: Mark DiChristina (© 2005, Mercy / Vineyard Publishing)

"God So Loved" (Worthy Is the Lamb That Was Slain"), words and music: Reuben Morgan (© 2000, Hillsong Publishing)

"Hail, Hail, the Lamb of God," words and music: John Barnett (© 1997, Mercy / Vineyard Publishing)

"Highly Exalted," words and music: Paul Baloche and Robin Mark (© 2007, Integrity's Hosanna! Music)

"Holy Lamb of God," words and music: Gary Sadler and Steven V. Taylor (© 2000, Integrity's Hosanna! Music)

"I Believe in a Hill Called Mount Calvary," words: Doug Oldham, Gloria Gaither, William J. Gaither, music: William J. Gaither (© 1968, William J. Gaither)

"Lamb of God," words and music: Twila Paris (© 1985, Straightway Music, Mountain Spring Music)

"Perfect Lamb of God," words and music: Adam Sacks (© 2004, Sovereign Grace Worship)

"Sweetly Broken" ("At the cross You beckon me..."), words and music: Jeremy Riddle (© Mercy / Vineyard Publishing)

"Ten Thousand Angels" ("He could have called..."), words and music: Ray Overholt (© 1959, renewed 1987, Lillenas Publishing Co.)

"The Blood Will Never Lose It's Power," words and music: Andraé Crouch (© 1966, Manna Music, Inc.)

"The Power of the Cross," words and music: Keith Getty and Stuart Townend (© 2005, Thankyou Music)

"This Is Love" ("I bow down to the Holy One..."), words and music by Mike Young and Terry Butler (© 1998, Mercy / Vineyard Publishing)

"This Man," words and music: Jeremy Camp (© 2004, Thirsty Moon River Publishing)

"The Wonders of His Hands," words and music: Geron Davis (© 1996, Integrity's Hosanna! Music)

"Unfailing Love," words and music: Jonathan Stockstill (© 2006, Integrity's Praise! Music)

"Via Dolorosa, Down the," words and music: Billy Luz Sprague and Niles Borop (© 1983, Meadowgreen Music Co.)

"Why?" words and music by Michael Card (© 1984, Mole End Music)

"Worthy the Lamb," words: Gloria and William J. Gaither, music: William J. Gaither (© 1974, William J. Gaither)

"Worthy Is the Lamb of God," words and music: Thomas Jackson (© 1991, Integrity's Hosanna! Music)

"You Are My All in All" ("Jesus, Lamb of God"),
   words and music: Dennis Jernigan (© 1991,
   Shepherd's Heart Music)

"You Deserve" ("Savior on a hill dying for my
   shame"), words and music: Darlene Zschech (©
   2004, Hillsong Publishing.